Bugle, Fife, And Drum Signals And Calls: As Used In The Regular Army And Militia Of The United States

Oliver Ditson And Company Publisher

BUGLE, FIFE, AND DRUM

SIGNALS AND CALLS,

AS USED IN THE

REGULAR ARMY AND MILITIA OF THE UNITED STATES.

NEW AND CORRECT EDITION.

BOSTON

OLIVER DITSON COMPANY.

NEW YORK: CHICAGO: PHILA: BOSTON:
C. H. Ditson & Co. Lyon & Healy, I. E. Ditson & Co. John C. Haynes & Co.

INTRODUCTORY.

On August 1st., 1867, the War Department ordered that "Upton's Tactics" be adopted by the Army of the United States, and by the Militia, as standard authority in place of all others. These tactics provide uniformity of system in all branches of the service, and therefore many changes have been made, which will hardly be recognized by the old soldier of twenty years ago.

The bugle (or trumpet) signals and calls, as well as those of the fife and drum, have consequently undergone a change like the other systems, and are now *the same* in all branches of the service, excepting such signals as pertain to some individual act of the cavalry or artillery soldier which cannot be performed by the infantryman. The general calls are the same throughout the army, according to "Upton's Tactics."

In this new book we give these calls, together with the *old ones* that were in use during the civil war, and feel confident that we have provided a correct and useful collection.

We are under obligations to D. Appleton & Co., publishers of "Upton's Army Tactics", for permission to use the new calls.

OLIVER DITSON & CO.

Boston, October, 1887.

_85157

BUGLE SIGNALS.

INFANTRY.

To economize space, the music is written an octave higher than the trumpet scale, and is adjusted to the scale of the bugle.

1.—ASSEMBLY OF BUGLERS.

Quick.

2.—ASSEMBLY.

Moderate.

(5)

3.—REVEILLE.

4.—RETREAT. *(One or three Bugles.)*

INFANTRY SIGNALS.

5.—TATTOO.

6.—EXTINGUISH LIGHTS.

Slow.

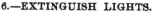

7.—MESS.

Quick.

8.—SICK.

Quick.

9.—SCHOOL.

10.—CHURCH.

11.—DRILL.

12.—FATIGUE.

13.—RECALL.

Moderate.

14.—ASSEMBLY OF GUARD DETAILS.

Quick.

15.—DRESS PARADE OR DRESS GUARD MOUNTING.

Quick.

16.—ADJUTANT'S CALL.

Quick.

17.—OFFICER'S CALL.

Quick.

18.—FIRST SERGEANT'S CALL.

Quick.

19.—THE GENERAL.

20.—TO ARMS.

21.—FIRE ALARM.

22.—ROGUES' MARCH.

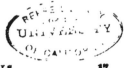

23.—FUNERAL MARCH.

Very slow.

Repeat at will.

24—PRESIDENT'S MARCH.

Quick time.

25—GENERAL'S MARCH.

Quick time.

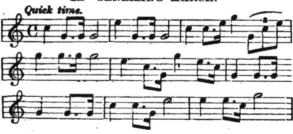

26.—FLOURISH FOR REVIEW.

Quick.

27.—TO THE COLOR.

Quick time.

END.

D.C.

28.—QUICKSTEP. No. 1.

Quick time.

29.—QUICKSTEP. No. 2.

30.—QUICKSTEP. No. 3.

31.—QUICKSTEP. No. 4.

F TRUMPET.

C CROOK.

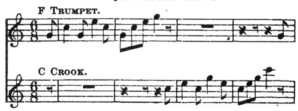

32.—QUICKSTEP, No. 5.

D.C.

33.—ATTENTION.
Slow.

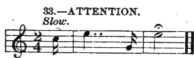

34.—FORWARD.

35.—HALT.

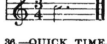

36.—QUICK TIME.

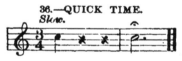

37.—DOUBLE TIME.

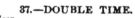

38.—CHARGE.

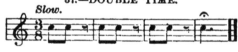

39.—GUIDE RIGHT.

Slow.

40.—GUIDE LEFT.

Slow.

41.—GUIDE CENTER.

Slow.

42.—FOURS RIGHT.

Slow.

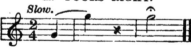

43.—FOURS LEFT.

Slow.

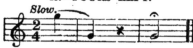

44.—FOURS RIGHT ABOUT.

45.—FOURS LEFT ABOUT.

46.—COLUMN RIGHT.

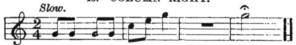

47.—COLUMN LEFT.

48.—RIGHT OBLIQUE.

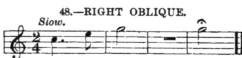

49.—LEFT OBLIQUE.

50.—RIGHT FRONT INTO LINE.

Moderate.

51.—LEFT FRONT INTO LINE.

Moderate.

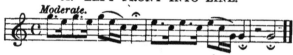

52—FACE TO THE REAR.

Slow.

53.—ON RIGHT INTO LINE.

Moderate.

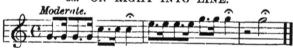

54.—ON LEFT INTO LINE.

Moderate.

55.—COMPANY RIGHT WHEEL.

56.—COMPANY LEFT WHEEL.

57.—COMMENCE FIRING.

58.—CEASE FIRING.

59.—SKIRMISHERS ATTENTION.

Slow.

60.—DEPLOY.

Quick.

61.—TO THE REAR.

Quick.

62.—BY THE RIGHT FLANK.

Moderate.

63.—BY THE LEFT FLANK.

Moderate.

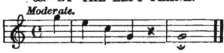

64.—RALLY BY FOURS.

65.—RALLY BY COMPANY.

66.—LIE DOWN.

67.—RISE UP.

CAVALRY SIGNALS.

1.—ATTENTION.

2.—MOUNT.

3.—DISMOUNT.

4.—WALK.

5.—TROT.

6.—GALOP.

7.—STABLE.

8.—WATERING.

9.—BOOTS AND SADDLES.

10.—PLATOONS RIGHT WHEEL.

11.—PLATOONS LEFT WHEEL.

12.—RALLY BY PLATOON.

13.—RALLY BY COMPANY.

☞ *All other calls and signals same as Infantry.*

ARTILLERY SIGNALS.

1.—ATTENTION.

2.—DRIVERS MOUNT.

3.—DRIVERS DISMOUNT.

4.—CANNONEERS MOUNT.

5.—CANNONEERS DISMOUNT.

6.—REVERSE.

7.—COUNTERMARCH.

8.—PLATOONS RIGHT WHEEL.

9.—PLATOONS LEFT WHEEL.

10.—IN BATTERY.

11.—BOOTS AND SADDLES.

12.—WATERING.

13.—STABLE.

14.—WALK.

15.—TROT.

16.—GALOP.

17.—BATTERY RIGHT WHEEL.

18.—BATTERY LEFT WHEEL.

☞ *All other signals same as Infantry.*

DRUM AND FIFE SIGNALS.

EXPLANATIONS.

t indicates tap; *f*, fiam; *d*, drag; *r*, roll. The figures under the rolls indicate the number of strokes in each roll. Continuous roll,

1.— THE GENERAL.

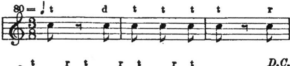

3.— THE ASSEMBLY.

3.—TO THE COLOR.

4.—THE LONG ROLL.

5.—THE REVEILLE.

120 = ♩ *Austrian.*

140 = ♩ *Hessian.*

DOUBLE DRAG.

DRUM.

D.C. the first part of the Reveille

6.—THE TROOF

7.—THE RETREAT.

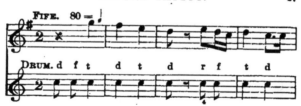

Play an Air in *Quick time* — after it, begin the Doubling.
Then an Air in *Common time* — after it, repeat the Doubling.
Then an Air in *Slow time* — and repeat the Doubling.
Finally an Air in *Double time*, followed by three Rolls.

After the three

Rolls repeat

Doubling

to the End.

9.—TO RECALL DETACHMENTS.

10.—DRUMMER'S CALL.

11.—COME FOR ORDER.

FIRST SERGEANTS.   3 times over.

SERGEANTS.   3 times over.

CORPORALS.   3 times over.

12.—CEASE FIRING.

OLD

ᴐALLS ᴬᴺᴰ SIGNALS,

As used previous to the Adoption of
Upton's Tactics in 1867.

EXPLANATION OF THE SIGNS.

MOVEMENT OF THE METRONOME.

76 — ♩ — 🎼 4 — or 76 steps to the minute.

80 — ♩ — 🎼 3 — or 80 steps to the minute.

100 — ♩· — 🎼 6/8 — or a 100 steps to the minute.

120 — ♩ — 🎼 2 — or a 120 steps to the minute.

Silence · · 𝄽 — Demi-silence. · · ·

GENERAL CALLS.

1.—ATTENTION.

120 — ♩ Allegro.

2.—THE GENERAL.

3.—THE ASSEMBLY.

4.—TO THE COLOR.

5.—THE RECALL.

6.—QUICK TIME.

7.—DOUBLE QUICK TIME.

165 = ♩ *Allegro.*

8.—THE CHARGE.

9.—THE REVEILLE

10.—RETREAT.

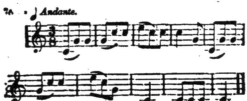

11.—TATTOO.

12.—TO EXTINGUISH LIGHTS.

76 = ♩ *Allegro.*

13.—ASSEMBLY OF THE BUGLERS.

40 = ♩ *Presto.*

14.—ASSEMBLY OF THE GUARD

118 = ♩ *Allegro.*

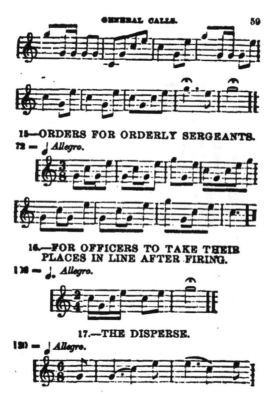

15—ORDERS FOR ORDERLY SERGEANTS.

72 = ♩ *Allegro.*

16.—FOR OFFICERS TO TAKE THEIR PLACES IN LINE AFTER FIRING.

1 36 — ♩. *Allegro.*

17.—THE DISPERSE.

1 30 — ♩ *Allegro.*

18.—OFFICERS' CALL.

152 = ♩. *Allegro.*

19.—BREAKFAST CALL.

138 = *Allegro.*

20.—DINNER CALL

21—SICK CALL.

22.—FATIGUE CALL.

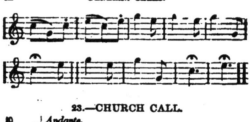

23.—CHURCH CALL.

24.—DRILL CALL.

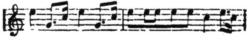

25.—SCHOOL CALL.

110 = ♩ *Allegro.*

CALLS FOR SKIRMISHERS.

1.—FIX BAYONET.

2.—UNFIX BAYONET.

3.—QUICK TIME.

(Music the same as in "General Calls.").

4.—DOUBLE QUICK TIME.

6.—DEPLOY AS SKIRMISHERS.

7.—FORWARD.

8.—IN RETREAT.

9.—HALT.

10.—BY THE RIGHT FLANK.

11.—BY THE LEFT FLANK.

12.—COMMENCE FIRING.

13.—CEASE FIRING.

80 — ♩ *Maestoso.*

14.—CHANGE DIRECTION TO THE RIGHT.

110 — ♩ *Allegro.*

15.—CHANGE DIRECTION TO THE LEFT.

110 — ♩ *Allegro.*

16.—LIE DOWN.

80 — ♩ *Moderato.*

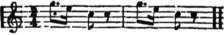

17.—RISE UP.

18.—RALLY BY FOURS.

19.—RALLY BY SECTIONS.

20.—RALLY BY PLATOONS.

21.—RALLY ON THE RESERVE.

76 = ♩ *Andante.*

22.—RALLY ON THE BATTALION.

76 = ♩ *Andante.*

23.—ASSEMBLE ON THE BATTALION.

90 = ♩ *Andante.*

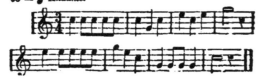

INDEX.

CPSIA information can be obtained
at www.ICGtesting.com
Printed in the USA
BVHW092025090223
658206BV00011B/1210